HOW TO STAY MARRIED

Jilly Cooper

How to
STAY MARRIED

ILLUSTRATED BY TIMOTHY JAQUES

TAPLINGER PUBLISHING COMPANY
NEW YORK

First Published in the United States in *1970* by
TAPLINGER PUBLISHING CO., INC.
New York, New York

Copyright © 1970 by Jilly Cooper

International Standard Book Number 0–8008–3981–1

Library of Congress Catalog Card Number 72–121666

Designed by Charles Kaplan

Printed in the United States of America

CONTENTS

FOR LEO

INTRODUCTION

It is extremely easy to get married—it costs a couple of dollars and takes two days to get a license. It is much harder to *stay* married.

My only qualifications for writing a book on the subject are that I have had the example of parents who have lived in harmony for nearly forty years, and I myself am still married extremely happily after nine years. In nine years, of course, we've had marvelous patches and patches so bad they rocked our marriage to its foundations, but I've come to realize that if you can cling on like a barnacle during the bad patches, your marriage will survive and in all probability be strengthened.

Anyone else's marriage is a dark unexplored continent, and although I have observed far too many of my friends going swiftly in and out of wedlock, I can only guess at what it was that broke the marriage up. Since the word got around that I was writing this book, my task has been made doubly difficult by the fact that married couples either sidled away or started behaving ostentatiously well, whenever I came into the room.

The trouble with most books on marriage, I think, is that they take the whole performance so humorlessly:

"The purpose of marriage," says one widely praised manual for young people, "is to regulate sexual conduct, to provide the domestic necessities of a household, to create a family by begetting the next generation, and to provide an atmosphere in which the capacity to love, and the desire for training and education lead into responsible adulthood. A good marriage demands constant work, etc., etc.," which is enough to send anyone contemplating marriage screaming to join the nearest celibate order.

They seem to forget that marriage can be fun—ours is. A sense of humor is the best way to deal with most problems, and for a marriage to be really successful your spouse should be your best friend as well as your lover.

One of the great comforts of my own marriage, however, has been that my husband was married before, knew the ropes, and during any really black period, when I was all for opting out and packing my bags, would reassure me that such black periods were to be expected in marriage, and that it had been far worse for him the first time round.

Similarly, I hope that by pointing out some of the disasters and problems that beset us and recalling how we weathered them, I may reassure other people, either married or contemplating marriage.

HERE COMES THE BRIDE

THE WEDDING

This is blast-off—the day you (or rather your mother) have been waiting for all your life. It'll pass in a dream and afterwards you won't remember a thing about it. It helps, however, if you both turn up. Dope yourself with tranquilizers by all

Bride not looking her best

means, but watch the champagne later: drugs mixed with drink often put you out like a light. And don't forget to take the price tags off your new shoes; they'll show when you kneel down in church.

Brides: don't be disappointed if you don't look your best. Far more likely you'll be scarlet in the face and piggy-eyed from lack of sleep.

Bridegrooms: remember to look round and smile as your bride comes up the aisle. She'll be too busy coping with her bouquet and veil to notice, but it will impress those armies of guests lined up on either side of the church.

Coming down the aisle's more tricky—you never know where to look—that radiant smile can easily set into a moronic grin—and there's bound to be one guest you know too well, whose eye you want to avoid (Tallulah Bankhead remarked about one couple coming down the aisle: "I've had them both and they were lousy!").

If you look solemn, people will think you're having second thoughts. Best policy is to settle for a cool smirk with your eyes on the door of the church.

Be careful what hymns you choose. People like a good bellow at a wedding, so don't choose anything obscure. Be equally careful of hymns with double meanings like, "Jesu—the very thought of thee," which will make everyone giggle and spoil the dignity and repose of the occasion.

THE RECEPTION

First there's the line-up, and you'll get so tired of shaking hands, trying to remember faces and gushing like an oil well, you'll begin to have real sympathy with the Royal Family.

Don't worry when you circulate among the guests afterwards if none of them will speak to you. They'll all feel you're far too important to waste time talking to them, and you'll wander round like a couple of lost souls.

If you must make speeches, keep them short. Thank everyone in sight, and tell one stunning joke to convince your in-laws you *do* have a sense of humor after all. Never let the best man either speak or read the telegrams.

Don't flirt with exes. One girl I know, whose husband spent the reception playing "do you remember" with an old girlfriend, refused to go on the honeymoon.

Try not to get drunk—you may feel like it, but it will cause recriminations later.

THE HONEYMOON

Originally, the honeymoon was intended for husbands to initiate their innocent young brides into the delights and mysteries of sex. Today, when most couples have slept together anyway and are already bankrupted by the cost of setting up a house, the whole thing seems a bit of a farce and a needless expense. You probably both need a holiday, however.

When you arrive at your destination, you're likely to feel a sense of anticlimax. You're exhausted and suffering from post-champagne depression (a real killer). For months you've been coping with squabbles with the caterers, bridesmaids' tantrums over their gowns, parcels arriving every day, the hall littered with packing straw, writer's cramp from answering letters, traumas with the bridal shop—every moment's been occupied, you're wound up like a clock, and suddenly it's all over and you've nothing to do for a couple of weeks except each other.

For the wife in particular, everything's suddenly new and unfamiliar, her new overnight case, new pigskin luggage, a whole trousseau of new clothes, dazzling white underwear instead of the usual dirty gray—even her name is new.

The thing to remember is that your spouse is probably as nervous and in need of reassurance as you are, like the wild beast surprised in the jungle who's always supposed to be more frightened than oneself.

SABOTEURS

The first thing to do on arrival at your honeymoon hotel is to search the bedroom for signs of sabotage. Practical jokers may well have instructed the hotel staff to make you an apple pie bed, or to wire up the springs of the bed to the hotel fire alarm.

One couple I know reached their hotel only to be confronted by the manager waving a telegram from one such joker saying: "My wife has just run off with my best friend. I believe they are booked into your hotel under the assumed name of Mr. and Mrs. So and So. Could you refuse to let them have the booked room until I arrive."

Whether you're heading for the Bahamas or Niagara Falls, the best way to scotch honeymoon saboteurs is not to be coy about your destination. Simply tell everyone you're staying at the Grand and then book rooms at the Majestic.

Then there's the problem of getting used to living together. Here again the wife in particular will be worried about keeping up appearances. Before marriage she's relied on nightly mud packs and rollers and skinfood, but now her husband's going to be with her every moment of the day, and the mystery's going to be ruined. When is she going to find time to shave her legs? And she's always told her husband she's a natural blonde, and suddenly he's going to find the peroxide in her suitcase.

She'll soon get used to it all, just as she'll get used to sitting on the john and gossiping to her husband while he's having a bath, or to wandering around with nothing on instead of discreetly changing in the bathroom.

If she's ashamed of her small breasts and mottled thighs, he's probably equally self-conscious about his narrow shoulders and hairless chest.

FIRST THING IN THE MORNING

If you're worried you look like a road accident in the morning, sleep with the curtains drawn, and if you're scared your mouth will taste like a parrot's cage when he bends over to kiss you, pretend you're going to the john, and nip out and clean your teeth.

DON'T PANIC if you get bored, or have a row, or feel claustrophobic or homesick. These are all part of growing-together pains. They won't establish a behavior pattern for the next fifty years.

A vital honeymoon ploy is to go somewhere where there is plenty to do. It's not sacrilege to go to the movies or watch a football game or even to

If she's ashamed . . .

look up friends in the district. Take lots of books and sleeping pills.

DON'T PANIC if you get on each other's nerves. My mother, who's been happily married to my father for nearly forty years, almost left him to enjoy the honeymoon alone because he got a line of doggerel on his mind and repeated it over and over again as they motored through the cornfields of France: *"C'est magnifique, Madame, c'est magnifique!"*

We drove around Norfolk on our honeymoon and I nearly drove my husband insane by exclaim-

18

ing: "How very lovely," every time we passed a village church.

SEX

I'm not going into the intricacies of sexual initiation—there are numerous books on the subject—I would just plead for both parties to be patient, tolerant, appreciative, and understanding. Temporary frigidity and impotence are not infrequent occurrences on honeymoon, and are not to be taken too seriously.

Take things slowly, you've probably got a lifetime in front of you—all that matters at this stage is to get across strong that you love each other, and that you're not sorry you're married.

Don't worry if, unlike the girl in *The Carpetbaggers* who wanted to see nothing but ceilings on her honeymoon, you don't feel like leaping on each other all the time. As I've already pointed out, you're probably exhausted and in no condition for a sexual marathon.

Do take a red towel if you're a virgin, or likely to be indisposed. It saves embarrassment over the sheets.

Even if you've been sleeping together for ages beforehand, and sex was stunning, don't worry if it goes off for a bit, or feel convinced that it can only work in a clandestine setting. You haven't been married before, and may just be suffering

19

from initial panic now that the stable door is well and truly bolted.

One friend told me he was awakened in the middle of most nights of his honeymoon by his wife staggering groggily out of bed, groping for her clothes and muttering she must get home before her parents woke up.

It's a good idea to borrow someone's cottage in the country for a honeymoon. It's cheaper than a hotel, and you won't be worried by the imagined chortlings of chambermaids and bellhops, and you can cook if you get bored.

Don't worry if he doesn't gaze into your eyes all the time and quote poetry. Most people don't know

Eases tension

enough poetry to last more than fifteen minutes. A certain amount of alcohol is an excellent idea—it eases tension and breaks down inhibitions. Take the case of the girl in our office who, on her arrival with her new husband at the hotel, was presented with a bottle of champagne.

"It was wonderful," she told us. "We shared a glass each night and made the bottle last the whole fortnight."

WEDDING PRESENTS

Get your thank-you letters written before the wedding. Once the pre-wedding momentum has been lost, you'll never get down to them.

Don't beef too much about the presents your partner's family or friends have given you, even if they are ghastly. No one likes to be reminded that they are related to, or acquainted with, people of execrable taste. Try and keep a list of who gave you what, so you can bring those cake forks out of hiding when Aunt Agatha comes to tea, and so you won't, as we did, give a particularly hideous vase back to the woman who gave it to us, when later she got married.

SETTING UP HOUSE

MOVING IN

At best a nightmare—as Dorothy Parker put it, the one dependable law of life is that everything is always worse than you thought it was going to be.

When my parents moved into their first house, they arrived to find the electricians had all the floor boards up, the paint was wet in the kitchen, and there was an enormous pile of rubble in the garage crowned by a one-horned, one-eyed stag.

Try therefore to get all major structural alterations done beforehand. Nothing is more depressing than trying to get a place straight with builders trooping in and out with muddy feet and demands for endless cups of coffee. Even the smallest job will seem as though they're building the Pyramids.

Try to get shelves up beforehand; moving men unpack at a fantastic rate, and you'll soon find every inch of floor space covered, with nowhere to put anything. Don't forget to get the gas and electricity turned on. Buy plenty of light bulbs.

Make a plan of where everything is going—or you'll end up with the grand piano in the bathroom, the refrigerator in the bedroom, and two angry movers buckling under the sideboard while you have a ferocious argument about where to put it.

Get some food in. You'll be so busy, you won't realize that the stores have closed, and so bankrupted after tipping the movers and rushing out to buy picture wire, screws, and plugs, that you won't have any money left to go out to dinner.

A bottle of whisky is an excellent soother of nerves—but don't let your moving men get their hands on it, or you'll have all your furniture scratched. A friend who had two particularly surly brutes made them a cup of coffee and slipped two amphetamines into each mug. After that she had one of the jolliest moves imaginable.

Do measure the height of the rooms before you go out and buy furniture at a sale. We had a tallboy standing in the street for weeks because we couldn't get it through any of the doors.

If possible, one of you should take a week off from work (even if it is unpaid) to get things in order. Nothing is more demoralizing than to come home late for the next month and face the chaos.

Try to get the kitchen and one other room habitable. Then you can shut yourselves away from the debris when it becomes too much for you.

If in the chaos of getting married, you are clever enough to find a suitable house, try and visit it at least twice before you buy, the first time when the owner has presumably gotten the place all spruced up for your visit, the second when she hasn't had time to put the child's rocking horse in front of the damp patch, or to put an armchair over the huge hole in the livingroom carpet.

Try and make the second visit in the morning; under artificial lighting, the dirtiest, most dilapidated house can look in good condition. Watch out, too, if the owner is drenched in perfume every time you visit the house; she may be trying to conceal the smell of faulty drains.

When you're newly married, there are two tremendous advantages in renting an apartment. A good super will do all those boring jobs like fixing fuses, regulating the heating, and keeping an eye on things while you're away.

And you won't have to bother about the upkeep of the exterior, either: blocked drains, holes in the roof, redecorating, etc. There's no garden waiting reproachfully every week end for your attentions, and there is the blessed anonymity of not having to live your lives out in front of all the neighbors. And finally, for the working wife, a small apartment is much easier to run than a house.

PETS

It goes without saying that if you want to keep pets, life is much easier in a house. It's not much fun having to take a dog down twenty floors in the elevator and across the road to the park every time it wants to go out, particularly if the dog from the

Pets in apartments

penthouse apartment is already in the elevator and fights with your dog all the way down.

A friend of ours was legally ejected from her New York apartment recently for keeping, in the words of her landlord's lawyers, "eleven cats, two Alsatians, and other nuisances."

We weren't allowed to have pets in our apartment when we were first married, and when the landlord made his annual inspection, the cats were always locked in the wardrobe. One year, however, the senior cat got his head stuck inside an elastic-sided boot which he kept bashing against the closet door, necessitating frenzied coughing, jumping up and down, and humming by my husband to cover up the noise. The landlord later described us as that nice girl with the strange husband.

DO-IT-YOURSELF

One of the great myths of marriage—heavily promoted by television commercials of smiling young couples up on ladders—is that home decorating is fun when you do it together.

It isn't. It's paralyzingly boring and caused more rows in our marriage than anything else. Just remember that, like having a brace on your teeth as a child, it's worth it later on.

Invariably one partner is more clumsy than the other, and the trouble starts when the more dexterous one becomes irritated and starts bossing poor hamfisted about. Hamfisted gets more and more sulky until a fight breaks out.

My husband is a great deal more adept than I am at decorating, but even so it was always a case of Wreck-it-Yourself. Our first attempts at wallpapering outcrazied the Crazy Gang. We lost our tempers, the yardstick and the scissors. I had bought enough paper to do two rooms (wildly expensive at thirty dollars a roll) but we had to scrap so much we only managed three quarters of one room. Finally, when we stood back to admire our wrinkled, uneven labors, we found we had papered the cat to the wall like the Canterville Ghost.

A FEW POINTS TO REMEMBER
Buy cheap wallpaper for your first attempts.

When you strip wallpaper and come to a layer of silver paper, leave it alone, or you'll find you've stripped off the insulation, and any paper subsequently put on the wall will turn green.

PAINTING
Do remember to put dust sheets down when you're painting or you'll get shortsighted aunts commenting on the attractive speckled border round the walls.

If you're doing the landing and the hall don't, as we did, start painting the landing scarlet, and the hall indigo—it never entered our heads that the colors would have to meet somewhere, in this case halfway up the stairs. The result was horrible.

Go to a showroom where you can see the paint you choose in large quantities. That color that looks so subtle on the color card can spread to vast deserts of ghastliness once it gets up on the wall.

The Canterville Cat

Don't mix paints unless you're an expert: they always come out sickly ice-cream shades.

Never get friends to help. Even your own pathetic attempts will be better than theirs. We let a girlfriend, who claimed she found painting therapeutic, loose on one of the spare rooms. When we looked in fifteen minutes later, there were terracotta flames of paint licking a foot high over the virgin white ceiling I had laborously painted the day before. None of our cries of "Steady on" or "I say" could halt her. The whole room had to be painted again.

Tell your wife before you paint a shelf or she'll bustle in five minutes later and replace everything you removed. You are bound to have a row about who didn't wash the brushes last time.

If you run out of paint, do remember the name and brand before you chuck the can away. We had to buy five different shades of orange before we hit on the right one again.

Lots of praise is essential. Say well done even if it isn't people get inordinately proud of the four square feet of wall they've just painted.

MISCELLANEOUS

Curtains were another disaster zone—in an attempt not to make them too short, I made them miles too long, so they trailed on the floor like a child dressing up in its mother's clothes. And of course there wasn't enough material left over for the valances.

Don't be fooled by do-it-yourself tiling kits: they're easy enough until you have to round a corner or meet a natural hazard like a light switch.

WORKMEN

Despite the hazards and boredom of home decorating and doing-it-yourself, I'm not sure it isn't preferable to having workmen in the house, particularly if they're doing structural alterations as well. You'll always find that the builders are waiting for the plumbers, who are waiting for the electricians, who're waiting for the carpenters, who in turn are waiting for the heating man, who in his turn is waiting for the builders. And as you're paying all of them while they hang about, you'll soon find there's a hole in your pocket, dear Eliza. It's like putting on a Broadway play; you never manage to get the right script, the right actors, an available theater, and financial backing all at the same time.

PEEPHOLES

In these days of violence, if you live in an apartment, it's essential to have a peephole cut in the door. One married girlfriend, whose husband had lost his latchkey, wouldn't let him in for two hours because she thought he might be a burglar. The door was so thickly padded and barred that she couldn't distinguish his voice, and all she could hear was violent banging and shouting.

TRADITIONAL ROLE OF HUSBAND AND WIFE

Traditionally the husband is the more practical

and mechanically-minded member of the team. But if he's the kind who hits the electricity cable every time he knocks a nail in, and puts up shelves crooked, and if his wife is the practical type who won honors in shopcraft at school, she shouldn't hesitate to take over. As my husband remarked, here was one sphere in which he wouldn't have minded having his masculinity undermined.

RUNNING THE HOUSE

HOUSEKEEPING

A major problem for the newly married wife, particularly if she is holding down a nine-to-five job. Before she was married she blew her wages on clothes and took her washing home to mother every week end. Now, suddenly, she must be housekeeper, cook, hostess, laundress, seamstress, beguiling companion, glamour girl, assistant bread-winner and willing bedfellow all in one.

What she must try and remember when she gets home exhausted from the office to be faced with a mountain of dirty dishes in the sink, the dinner to be cooked, the bed to be made, the flat or house to be cleaned, a pile of shirts to be ironed, and her husband in a playful mood, is that where marriage is concerned, CHEERFULNESS, SEXUAL ENTHUSIASM, AND GOOD COOKING are far nearer to Godliness than cleanliness about the house.

So long as the apartment is kept tidy—men hate living in a muddle—meals are regular, and their wives are in good spirits, husbands won't notice a few cobwebs.

If you amuse a man in bed, he's not likely to bother about the mountain of dust underneath it.

RESENTMENT

If a wife feels resentful that she is slaving away while her husband comes home and flops down in front of the television until dinner is ready, she must remember that it isn't all roses for him either.

He has given up his much-prized bachelor status for marriage and he probably expects, like his father before him, to come home every night to a gleaming home, a happy wife, and a delicious dinner. Instead he finds a tearful, fractious shrew, and he forgets that his mother looked after his father so well because she didn't have to go out to work.

TOLERANCE

Tolerance is essential on both sides. If the wife is working the husband should be prepared to give her a hand. Equally, it's up to the wife to speak up when she needs help, and not to scurry round with a face set like someone out of the city morgue. As men hate seeing their wives slaving, one of the solutions is for the wife to get her housework done when her husband isn't around.

That housekeeping whizz-kid Mrs. Beeton suggests getting up early, and I managed to persuade most of my employers to let me work from eight-thirty to four-thirty. Eight-thirty sounds horrendous, but once you're used to it, it's much the same as nine. You miss the rush-hour traffic both ways, you have a nice quiet half-hour in the office before anyone else arrives in which to ring your mother or make a shopping list (no one knows whether you got in exactly at eight-thirty anyway), and you get home well before your husband so you have time to get dinner on, tidy up and welcome him home.

Another solution is to encourage your husband to have at least one night out a week with the boys. Then you have a few hours to catch up.

CLEANING WOMEN

Or you can employ a cleaning woman. If you get a good one, hang on to her, she's worth her weight in bullion. Generally, alas, maids start off marvelously and then after a few weeks the standard goes down and so does the level of the gin. My husband came home once and found ours asleep in our bed with the electric blanket and the radio on.

Asleep in our bed

If I have a good cleaning woman, I find I spend far more time than before tidying up before she comes, and if I get a bad one, I spend hours tidying up after her, so my husband won't grumble about throwing money away and force me to sack her.

They also have an irritating habit of not turning up on the day your mother-in-law is coming to stay, or when you're relying on them to tidy up before a large dinner party.

Our present one, as my husband says, comes in "to spread the dirt more evenly," and she does it very smartly.

But to return to housework. Remember that the dust you flick away today will have drifted back into place tomorrow. Once when I was rabbiting on about the dirtiness of my house, a girlfriend, whose house is none too clean either, told me I was suffering from the bourgeois syndrome: namely, obsessive worrying over spit and polish. It worked like a charm. I didn't do any housework for at least two weeks.

A FEW QUICK POINTERS

Have lots of cushions to hide things under when guests arrive, and plump them a great deal. The woman who has the tidiest house in London has huge arm muscles from plumping.

Closing untidy desks, straightening papers, putting books back vertically instead of horizontally,

Huge arm muscles

replacing records in their sleeves, and picking
things up off the floor, all make a room look better
quicker than dusting or vacuuming.

Empty ashtrays, clear dirty glasses into the
kitchen, open windows at night, or the place will
smell like a barroom in the morning.

Get a decent vacuum cleaner or you'll be like a
girlfriend who grumbled to her husband that she

was quite exhausted from cleaning all day. He looked around and said: "I wish you'd do some cleaning in our house for a change!"

Don't vacuum under his feet—it's grounds for divorce.

If your kitchen is a pigsty, don't have a glass door or a hatch through which inquisitive guests can peer.

Don't use all your dusting cloths for polishing silver or shoes or you'll have to hare round before dinner parties dusting furniture with the front of your dress the way I do.

LAUNDRY

If you can possibly afford it during the first six months, send your husband's shirts to the laundry. When I was first married, one of the things that nearly broke my back was washing and ironing seven shirts a week. Do encourage your husband to buy dark shirts for the office so he can wear them for at least two days.

If you wash at home, don't, as I always do, put in far too much soap powder and spend the next two hours rinsing.

If you wash at a self-service laundry, always remember to put your money into the machine or you'll come back forty minutes later only to find your clothes still unwashed. Be careful not to put any dark things that run in a white wash. When we were first married, I left in a red silk handkerchief. My husband's shirts came out streaked like the dawn, he wore cyclamen shorts for weeks and claimed he was the only member of his football team with a rose-pink jock strap.

If you have a spin dryer, remember to put a bowl under the drain pipe or you'll have the kitchen awash every time. Drying is a problem in a small apartment; one of the most useful presents we had was a portable electric dryer which will dry all the washing in about six hours.

Husbands are not amused by singe marks. They can be removed with peroxide, and in an emergency use talcum powder. Always put ironing away when you've finished—either the cat is bound to come and sit on it, or it looks so badly ironed it gets mistaken for dirty laundry and washed again.

The ideal, of course, is to send everything to the laundry. Unfortunately, our laundry is notorious for "losing" things and for not getting things back on time; we've grown quite accustomed to the rough male kiss of blankets.

CLEANING

Try to keep all cleaning tickets in one place. We always lose them, and at this moment, half our wardrobe is sitting in various cleaners' all over town, soon to be auctioned off.

FOOD

I got the sack from my first job after I was married because I spent all morning on the telephone apologizing to my husband for the row we'd had on the bus, and all afternoon reading recipe books.

Cooking well and cheaply is a major problem for the young wife. Before she was married she probably invited her fiancé to dinner from time to time and blew half her wages on heavy cream and brandy to go with the sirloin steak and shellfish, so that he is under the illusion that she is a marvelous cook. Now that she is married, she will find cooking exciting meals every evening—while not overtaxing her imagination or the family budget—extremely difficult.

Don't, however, be seduced into buying things that are cheap if they repel you. I once bought a black pudding because I was told it was inexpensive and nourishing. It lay like a long dark slug in the refrigerator for three weeks, finally turned green, died, and was duly committed to the garbage.

Strive for variety: however much he raves over your chicken pie, he won't want it twice a week for the next fifty years.

Buy in bulk if you and your husband have self-control: we find bulk buying never does anything but increase our bulk. The roast that is bought on Saturday never graduates into cold meat and later shepherd's pie. It is always wolfed in one sitting.

Buy in bulk

Once we made a big casserole to last a week. It took eight hours to cook, stank the whole apartment house out, and went bad the following day.

Leave long-cooking dishes for the week end. Nothing irks a man more than having to wait until midnight to eat. Do take the stew off the gas before you start making love.

Never hide things—you won't remember where you put them. I hid some potted shrimps once and discovered them a month later after we'd had the floor boards torn up.

HUSBANDS

If you find a half-bottle of wine in the kitchen, check before you drink it. Your wife may be saving it for cooking some exotic dish.

41

Don't be bossy in the kitchen. Nothing irritates a woman more than to be told to add some more paprika, or that your mother always made it with real mashed potato.

MONEY

Honesty about money is absolutely essential in marriage. If you are to avoid major rows, you must know how much money you've got in the bank, and how much each of you is spending.

In theory all bills should be kept together and paid at the end of each month. Weekly accounts should be kept and the financial situation should be reviewed every month.

In practice we never did any of these things. We both got married with overdrafts well into three figures—having lived at home I had no idea of the cost of living, and between us we were earning far less than we were spending. We ricocheted from one financial crisis to another.

Economizing is particularly hard when you're first married, for there are so many things to do to the house, and if the wife is determined to impress the husband with her cooking, it's cream and wine in everything.

What usually happened was that I would rush home early to make an anniversary dinner celebrating our marriage of exactly five weeks and three days. I would have just started cooking my husband's favorite meal, shrimp cocktail and a large T-bone steak, when he would stagger in the door and start rhapsodizing about the huge expense-account lunch he'd had that noon.

"What did you eat?" I'd ask him.

"Oh, shrimp cocktail and a T-bone steak, of course."

All the regular stores having closed, I'd have to rush out to the all-night delicatessen around the corner, where there were such ferocious mark-ups on everything that food for one single dinner would cost more than an entire week's housekeeping money.

We used to have absurd economy campaigns: drinking tea instead of coffee for breakfast, driving miles to find a station which sold cheaper gas, turning out the lights and creeping around in the dark to save electricity, smoking less (which meant we ate more), eating less (which meant we smoked more).

We did evolve a splendid bill-paying evasion technique. We never paid a thing until we got a dunning letter; then we would send the creditor a check, unsigned, so they would spend another week returning it, whereupon it would be returned in successive weeks, with the date left off, the wrong year, or the numbers and letters differing.

Another ruse was to ring up when the final reminder turned up and say in aggrieved tones:

"But I've already paid it." This ploy usually provided a month's grace while they tried to trace it.

With electricity, gas and telephone, you can always write and query the amount, saying you've been away for the last month and can't think why the bill is so high.

Perhaps the best method is to keep sending the bill back with "Not known here" written across it.

I once tried to keep our accounts and in the third week, when I was making great efforts to economize, I saw to my horror that our expenditures had doubled. I went sobbing to my husband, who pointed out quite kindly that I'd added in the date.

Try to pay your bills by the month—and why not investigate a household budget account with your bank manager? It simplifies bill-paying considerably. Another minor money problem is that one always assumes that one's partner will have some money on him, and he never has, so you find you can't take buses because neither of you can pay the fare, and walk home five miles from parties in the middle of the night because you can't afford a taxi.

Remember that each partner is bound to think the other one extravagant, and that everyone always thinks he is broke, however rich he is. As one friend said the other day: "We're just as poor today as when we were first married but on a much, much grander scale."

SHOPPING

Shop early in the morning when there's more of a selection, and mid-week, when things are cheaper.

As I've already said, avoid the stores that stay open late at night as they invariably put a huge mark-up on everything.

Always make a list, or you'll have the absurd experience of trailing blocks to shop for bargains during your lunch hour, only to end up at five o'clock spending a fortune at the fancy grocery for all the things you've forgotten.

Don't let men go near markets; they'll blow the month's rent on one meal and come home very smug because they've shopped so much more quickly than you would have done.

Take things out of your shopping bag and put them away at once or you'll have frozen raspberries melting on the livingroom carpet, and liver blood permanently stained on your checkbook.

Despite the maxim: "If you can get it on credit it's free, if you can pay by check it's almost free, but if you have to pay cash, it's bloody expensive," pay cash if you can. Our biggest shopping bill is always for drink because we can chalk it up at the liquor store round the corner.

Be tolerant of each other's extravagances. Everyone lapses from time to time. One of the nicest things about my husband is that he never grumbles about a new dress unless he thinks it's ugly.

GARDENING

Neither my husband nor I have a green thumb. We have only to look at a potted plant for it to shrivel on the spot, so when we moved into our house and had a garden to cope with, it became a millstone round our necks.

April is the cruelest month. Every year we look at each other dismally and say: "This year, we really must do something about the garden."

This year, in fact, it was worse than ever. One gray tablecloth had been flapping on the clothesline since October, and in January a Chinese friend gave a party at our house, and all the guests threw their spareribs out the window when they finished eating, so the garden now looks like Death Valley.

I suppose the answer would be to pave the whole thing over, but this is a bore later on when you have children because they're always falling over and cracking their heads.

If you have a lawn, you have to mow it occasionally. With us it's always a question of scything; my husband claims the smell of new-mown hay evokes the joys of his childhood.

The only thing that can be said for digging is that it's a good way to sober up if you've drunk too much the night before.

Don't, as we always do, put off buying your packets of seeds until May. When we get them home, the instructions on the back invariably recommend planting in early March, but we plant them late regardless. As a rule, our garden is just about ready to bloom by October, when the first frost usually kills everything stone dead.

TIDINESS AND UNTIDINESS

If you are married to a real slob, who constantly keeps the house in a mess and serves up vile food, you have every right to complain. There's a happy medium between being a doormat and a bully. Rather than work yourself into a frenzy of resentment, first try to tease your wife out of her sloppi-

A firm hand

ness, and if that doesn't work, risk a scene by telling her it just isn't good enough.

Women on the whole quite like a firm hand, and one of the saddest things a wife ever said to me was: "It was only on the day he left me that he told me for the first time that I was a lousy cook, I turned the place into a pigsty, I never ironed his shirts, and left mustard under the plates."

Men like a place they can relax in and if the wife is the tidy one, she shouldn't nag and fuss at her husband the moment he gets home.

"I can't stand it any longer," said one newly married husband. "She's taken all my books and put them in drawers like my shirts."

"Among some of the best marriages," my tame psychiatrist once told me, "are those in which, although the husband and wife started at relatively distant poles of neatness and sloppiness, man and wife gradually moved towards a common middle ground, through love, understanding and willingness to understand each other's needs."

"IF THERE'S ONE THING I CAN'T STAND..."

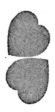

CHANGING PEOPLE

You shouldn't go into marriage expecting to change people. Once a bumbler always a bumbler, once a rake always a rake (a roving eye isn't likely to be doused by marriage). Once a slob—although she may make heroic and semi-successful attempts to improve—always a slob. When we were first married, my husband used to dream of the day I would stop working—like the Three Sisters yearning for Moscow: "The house will be tidy, we shall make love every morning, and at last I shall be given breakfast."

Well, I stopped work, and chaos reigned very much as usual. It's a case of *plus ça change,* I'm afraid.

Your only hope is that by making people happier and more secure they may realize the potential inside them and develop into brilliant businessmen, marvelous lovers, superb cooks, or alas, even bores. And remember, the wife who nags her husband into making a fortune won't see nearly so much of him. He'll be in the office from morn until night. She can't have it both ways.

DIFFERING TASTES

Certain things are bound to grate. He may have a passion for hunting prints and electronic gadgets and she may spend a bundle on plastic bulrushes and a chiming doorbell.

The wife may also use certain expressions like "Pleased to meet you," which irritate her husband to death; or he may say "What a generous portion" every time she puts his food in front of him.

Now is the time to strike. If you say you can't stand something in the first flush of love, your partner probably won't mind and will do something about it. If, after ten years, you suddenly tell your husband it drives you mad every time he says: "Sit ye down" when guests arrive, he'll be deeply offended, and ask you why you didn't complain before.

IRRITATING HABITS

Everyone has some irritating habits—the only thing to do when your partner draws your attention to them is to swallow your pride and be grateful, because they may well have been irritating everyone else as well.

I have given up smoking and eating apples in bed, or cooking in my fur coat, and I try not to drench the butter dish with marmalade. My husband no longer spends a quarter of an hour each morning clearing the frog out of his throat, and if

he still picks his nose, he does it behind a newspaper.

There are bound to be areas in your marriage
where you are diametrically opposed. Compromise
is the only answer. I'm cold blooded, my husband
is hot blooded. I sleep with six blankets, he sleeps
half out of the bed.

I like arriving late for parties so I can make an
entrance, he likes arriving on the dot because he
hates missing valuable drinking time. I can't count
the number of quiet cigarettes we've had in the
car, waiting for a decent time to arrive.

Don't worry too much that habits which irritate
you now will get more and more on your nerves.
My tame psychiatrist again told me: "Those quirks
in one's marriage partner which annoy one in early
days often become in later years the most lovable
traits."

ROWS

My husband and I quarrel very seldom, we both loathe rows and hate being shouted at. I was very worried when I first married because I read that quarreling was one of the most common methods of relieving tensions in marriage, and was confronted with the awful possibility that our marriage had no proper tensions.

It is very hard to generalize about rows. Some of the happiest married people I know have the most blazing rows, and then make it up very quickly— like lawyers who argue heatedly in court all day and then meet on terms of utter amicability in the bar five minutes later.

However much a good fight clears the air, one is bound during its course to say something vicious and hurtful, which may well be absorbed and brooded upon later. Try therefore to cut rowing down to the minimum. It will upset children when they come along, and if you row in public, it's boring and embarrassing for other people, and you won't get asked out any more.

We found the occasions when rows were most likely to break out were:

Friday night—both partners are tired at the end of the week.

Sunday afternoon—both partners are slightly bored because there's nothing exciting happening, they're also feeling guilty because they haven't done anything worthwhile like painting the bathroom, and depression about Monday morning is already setting in.

After parties—be careful of this one—an awful lot of very nasty and unforgettable home truths can come out if one or both of you is tight.

Going away for week ends—one person is always ready and anxious to avoid the rush-hour, the other is frantically packing all the wrong things, so the first five miles of the journey will be punctuated with cries of "Oh God" and U-turns against the ever-increasing traffic to collect something forgotten.

Weddings—the minister's pep-talk in church on Christian behavior in marriage always sets us off on the wrong foot. Then afterwards we'll be suffering from post-champagne gloom and wondering if we're as happy as the couple who've just gotten married.

Television—husband always wants to watch boxing, and the wife a movie.

Desks—the tidy one will be irritated because the untidy one is always rifling the desk, and pinching all the stamps and envelopes.

Clothes—men not having a clean shirt, or clean shorts to wear in the morning.

Space in the bedroom—the wife will appropriate five and three quarters out of six of the drawers and three out of four of the coat hangers, and leave her clothes all over the only chair.

MINOR IRRITATIONS, ALL LIKELY TO CAUSE ROWS

The wife should avoid using her husband's razor on her legs and not washing it out, or cleaning the bathtub with his washcloth, or using a chisel as a screwdriver, or pinching the husband's sweaters. There are also the eighteen odd socks in her husband's top drawer, the rings of lipstick on his best handkerchief, running out of toothpaste, toilet paper, soap. Forgetting to turn out lights, fires, the oven. Forgetting to give her husband his letters or telephone messages.

My husband also drives me mad by always leaving his cuff links in his shirts and then grumbling because they get lost at the laundry. Then, too, he never realizes he hasn't taken a towel with him into the bathroom until he's actually in the bath, so I always have to put down what I'm doing, making toast or feeding the baby, and rush upstairs to get him one.

He also has another maddening habit—common to many men, I think—of wolfing down a huge late Sunday-morning breakfast: eggs, sausages, bacon, tomatoes, fried bread, toast, marmalade—the works. Then he grumbles that he's getting too fat, that I'm trying to push him into an early grave by overfeeding him, and that he doesn't, *absolutely doesn't* want another mouthful to eat for the rest of the week end.

Come four o'clock, he's nosing around the cookie jar, and by six o'clock he starts saying he's starving and what am I going to cook him for dinner!

MAKING UP

Never be too proud to apologize, but do it prop-

Poor Tibbles

erly, none of that "I've said I'm sorry, haven't I?" followed by a stream of abuse.

Don't worry about letting the sun go down on your wrath—it's no good worrying a row to its logical conclusion when you're both tired and then lying awake the rest of the night. Take a sleeping pill, get a good night's sleep and you'll probably have forgotten you ever had a row by morning.

Try not to harbor grudges and never stop speaking to each other.

A sense of humor is all-important for ending rows. My husband once in rare mid-row put both feet into one leg of his shorts and fell over, I went into peals of laughter and the row was at an end.

Once when I was threatening to leave him he looked reproachfully at the cat, and said: "But we can't let poor Tibbles be the victim of a broken home."

A NOTE ON FEMININE PROBLEMS

BLACK GLOOMS

Normally I am a pretty equable person, but in the first six months I was married, I suffered from the most fearful black glooms, and I have since discovered that many other women feel the same. I think these depressions are generally a reaction after the excitement of the wedding, and are also caused by complete exhaustion and feeling quite unable to cope with running a home, a job, and a new husband all at the same time.

These glooms are extremely tedious for the husband but mustn't worry him unduly unless they linger on longer than a few days. Nothing will be achieved by ordering the wife to snap out of it. Patience, lots of loving, and constant praise and encouragement are the only remedies.

THE CURSE

Should be renamed the blessing. Every row two weeks before it arrives, and a week after it's finished, can be blamed on it.

ANNIVERSARIES

Husbands are notorious for forgetting birthdays

and anniversaries. Don't expect a heart-shaped box of chocolates on Valentine's Day, but avoid a fight on other occasions by saying loudly about three days before: "What shall we do on my birthday/our anniversary on *Friday*, darling?"

CHRISTMAS

This row usually starts about September and continues through to February.

Wife: Where shall we go for Christmas, darling?

Husband: Anywhere you like, darling.

Wife: Well, I thought we might spend a few days with Mother.

Husband (appalled): With your mother! No booze, and frost because we don't go to church three times a day. If you think I'm staying with that old cow . . .

Wife (interrupting with some asperity): What did *you* have in mind?

Husband: Well, I rather thought we might go to Scotland.

Wife: To stay with your parents! No central heating, and those damned dogs—that's charming.

And the row follows its normal course.

Many people like to go to their families for Christmas and can't understand why their partners find it such a strain. If you can't stand going to either set of parents, get a large dog and say you can't leave it.

CHRISTMAS PRESENTS

These can be an awful bore, particularly if you

61

come from or marry into a large family. We've evolved a system whereby my husband buys all the men's presents and I look after the women and children.

Even so we've made some awful boners. A cousin of my husband's who's just had her house redecorated never forgave me for giving her youngest son a set of oil paints, and there was the awful occasion when I gave a rigidly teetotal aunt a bottle of cherry brandy.

Getting presents back is also tricky. One year an in-law gave me an orange sweater, and although orange is a color I detest, I hypocritically wrote back saying how delighted I was. Since then, every Christmas I've had a succession of orange hats, mufflers, and cardigans, orange beads and orange lipsticks, and I always have to remember to wear them when I go to visit her.

A friend of mine was given a hideous but wildly expensive clock by her mother-in-law. Although the friend wrote saying how absolutely thrilled she was, the fact is that she took the clock straight back to the store at which it was bought, and swapped it for exotic things like Russian cigarettes and imported chocolates.

Unfortunately, the store got the wrong end of the stick and instead of crediting these delightful luxuries in exchange for the clock, it promptly charged them to the mother-in-law's account. Bills for all these frivolities prompted a call to the unwary daughter-in-law, at which point the true story of the swapped clock had to come home. Diplomatic relations have since been severed.

RELATIONS AND FRIENDS

IN-LAWS

The ideal is to marry an orphan. However hard you try, you'll probably have some trouble with your in-laws. Mine have always been angelic to me but as my mother-in-law pointed out to me in a moment of candor, nobody is ever good enough to marry one's child.

Be kind to your in-laws. Remember that many parents are so involved with their children that they regard it as an act of treacherous infidelity when these children meet someone and love them enough to want to marry them. For years a mother has considered herself her son's "best girl" or her daughter's "best friend," then suddenly she's been ousted. She sees her ewe lamb confiding in someone else, and as they draw further and further away from her, she becomes more and more unpleasant by trying to hang on to them.

Tact is essential. Be particularly nice to your husband when his mother is around but don't neck, and don't exclude her with private jokes. A bit of buttering up doesn't go amiss. It's a good idea for a wife to ask her mother-in-law's advice about cooking and washing; tell her your husband is always raving about her apple pie, how does she make it?

On the other hand it's important for the husband to see that his mother doesn't move in on the household and take over. It's only too easy for a dominant mother-in-law to undermine the confidence of a young and inexperienced wife. Try and restrict her visits to the occasional week end once or twice a year, and if she shows signs of making a long stay, you can always say you've got an Aborigine lodger moving in at the end of the week, and as long as she doesn't mind sharing a bedroom with him . . .

Finally, there's not much point in trying to be anything other than yourself with your in-laws. You'll have to keep up the act a long time. I was so nervous when I first met my mother-in-law that when she asked me if I took sugar in my tea, I said yes without thinking, although I never do. Ever since then she's prided herself on remembering that I take sugar, and I have to force myself to drink revoltingly sweet tea.

One thing, however, that always seems to upset the older generation is heavy eye make-up and long untidy hair, so if you want to take the business of getting on with in-laws really seriously, it doesn't hurt to soft-pedal the make-up and tie back your hair when you see them.

The husband's best tack is to flirt with his mother-in-law, even if she's an old boot. Few women can resist flattery.

Wives can flirt with their fathers-in-law, but

Flirting with mother-in-law

don't overdo it, or you'll have your mother-in-law branding you a fast piece.

However much you dislike having your in-laws to stay, be philosophical about it: at least it will make you clean the place up. My mother-in-law once slept peacefully and unknowingly on a pillow-case full of wet-washing. Don't give them too lush food or they'll think you're being extravagant. Meat loaf, two vegetables, and a salad will impress them far more than lobster and caviar. And hide those battalions of empties before they arrive.

My husband always takes his parents on a tour of the house, pointing out things that need repairing, in anticipation of a fat check.

YOUR OWN PARENTS

However fond you are of your own parents, remember that when a man marries "he shall leave his father and mother and cleave unto his wife."

Loyalty to your husband or wife must always come first. Don't chatter to your mother too long or too often on the telephone. It will irritate your husband and possibly make him jealous.

If you have a fight with your husband or wife, and pack your bags, go to a discreet friend, never, never go home to your parents. You will say a lot of adverse things about your partner in the heat of the moment, which you will forget afterwards, but your parents will remember them and it will be extremely difficult afterwards for your parents and partner to pick up the threads again.

FRIENDS

A friend married is a friend lost, goes the proverb, and certainly one of the sad facts of marriage is that it's almost impossible to keep up with friends one's other half doesn't like. You can relegate them to lunch dates and evenings when your partner is out, but invariably they get the message and sweep off in low dudgeon.

Much of the first year of marriage is spent weeding out the sheep from the goats. Both parties should try not to be jealous of the other half's close friends. My husband certainly made short work of any friends he considered a) boring, b) unstable influences.

If you find your husband's friends a bore, establish a reputation for delicacy early on in the marriage. Then when they lurch in drunkenly from a pub, you can plead exhaustion and disappear upstairs to read a book.

Nothing irritates many husbands more than a good female gabfest: "You honestly think I can wear it without a bra? That junk clogs the pores . . . So she left him and went off with the dentist and the furniture . . . ?"

As my father once said to my mother: "I've nothing against other women, darling, except they make you so boring."

You may also find that girlfriends can be very jealous and bitchy. When we were first married, we were bursting with pride until a rich and unmarried friend came to tea. Peering around our sparsely furnished flat, she inquired: "I suppose all your furniture's still in storage?"

DROPPERS-IN

Ought to be abolished. People should telephone first and ask if you want to see them. No one will bother you the first month or so. They used to apologize to us for telephoning after seven o'clock, assuming we'd be in bed. After that they'll descend in droves, looking curiously for signs of strain in your faces, avid to see what kind of mess you've made of your apartment.

One method of getting rid of them is to dispatch your husband to the bedroom, rip off all your clothes, ruffle your hair, and, clad only in a face towel, answer the door brandishing the *Kama Sutra*. The droppers-in will be so embarrassed that they'll apologize and make themselves scarce.

Answering the door

ENTERTAINING NOTIONS

ENTERTAINING

Always check with your partner before you issue or accept an invitation, or you'll get ghastly instances of double dating.

Time and again recently, we've been making tracks for bed when the telephone rings and an irate voice says, "Aren't you coming? We're all waiting to go in to dinner." Or we'll be just leaving the house to go out, when a rosy-cheeked couple arrive on the doorstep, having driven in fifty miles from the country for dinner.

Keep a book by the telephone and write everything down.

DINNER PARTIES

Unless you're a Cordon Bleu cook, and totally unflappable, your first dinner parties are bound to be packed with incident. Overcooked meat, undercooked potato salad, soufflés that don't rise, guests that don't rise to the occasion.

If you're a beginner, cook as much as possible the day before. Fishballs, liver pâté, soup, casseroles and most desserts can all be made beforehand. Then all you have to do the following day is to make the toast and mix a salad dressing.

If possible, get the table ready the night before as well.

Polishing glasses, ironing napkins, getting out plates and coffee cups all take longer than one would imagine. Get plenty of cheese, in case you haven't given people enough to eat—I once fell down the stairs with a pudding and eight plates, and there was no cheese in the house.

Don't spend hours away from your guests. Nothing is less calculated to put them at their ease than a hostess who turns up red in the face after three-quarters of an hour, grabs a quick drink and disappears again.

Guests

One couple we had dinner with disappeared for an hour to peel grapes for the Sole Véronique, and the whole meal was served to an accompaniment of imitation whipped cream.

Be careful whom you ask with whom: the day our vicar's wife came to dinner we invited a young man who regaled us for half the evening with details of the mating habits of the rhinoceros.

There are other guests to be avoided:

The non-eater who pushes her food to one side of her plate after one mouthful and blows smoke in everyone's face.

The slow eater who insists on telling long stories and then finishing all his food.

The wife who rings up at the last moment and says, "Charles is hung over, may I bring my sister? It won't foul up your numbers, will it?"

The bachelors who specially ask you to fix them up with a divine girl, and when you do, spend the entire evening chatting up all the married women.

The couple who're going to a cocktail party first and arrive very drunk an hour late, then have a row, tell blue stories, and fall asleep immediately after dinner.

The woman your husband fancies. (There, the only solution is to serve her sweet corn or asparagus; no girl looks sexy with butter running down her chin.)

Don't become a slave to social ping-pong. Entertaining is wildly expensive and just because you had caviar and three kinds of wine at the Vander-Rocks, don't feel you have to give them oysters and liqueurs when they come back to you.

If you're broke, warn people beforehand that it will only be spaghetti and Spanish Burgundy; then they can either refuse, bring a bottle, or have a number of stiff drinks beforehand.

If you're worried about the food, drink for at least an hour and a half before you eat, and they'll be so tight they won't know what they're eating.

Equally, if you're supremely confident about your food, don't let them drink too much.

Don't play loud background music before dinner; it kills conversation. People can go to a concert if they want that sort of thing.

Never, never show slides.

How many evenings have we sat in other people's homes without drink or cigarettes, looking at indescribably boring slides of vacation trips? The running commentary: "Oh, this is one of the best, you *must* see this one, this is Elmer and me at— now where was it? That thing at the back? Oh, Notre Dame or the Tower of Pisa or something. Oh yes, and this, you must see this one. This is the back of Tommy's head and . . ."

Only twice have we ever enjoyed home movies: once at a children's party at which the father accidentally started showing one of his blue movies, and on one other occasion when our host screened seaside slides. Unfortunately, he forgot to remove

Home movies and ex-wives

a (very) candid shot of his first wife emerging from the sea as naked as the Botticelli Venus.

IF THEY WON'T GO

The husband should make the first move by saying his wife is tired and sending her to bed. If that doesn't work, turn the central heating off.

If you don't like certain people, don't feel you have to ask them back. They'll get the message eventually. Life is too short to bother with people you really don't care for. You'll work up too much tension beforehand about having to see them, and too much spleen afterwards about how bored you were.

PARTIES
Make a list and stick to it. We always ask indiscriminately and have far too many people, both of us trying to smuggle in people the other one doesn't like.

Don't send out invitations. You can't ask everyone, and people get very sour if they see your invitations on other people's mantelpieces. Also, if you invite by telephone, you get a "yes" or "no" immediately, and people are notoriously bad at answering letters.

We once gave a drears' sherry party—with fatal consequences. All our undreary friends found out and were furious they hadn't been invited, and the drears discovered why they'd been asked, and were deeply offended. We were a bit short of friends that year.

One of the secrets of a good party is a few abrasive elements. Recently we went to an outstandingly successful "bring-an-enemy" party.

Don't expect to enjoy your own parties, except in retrospect. All your guests will be too busy getting drunk and trying to make other guests to bother about you. Your function is to act as unpaid waiter and waitress: effecting introductions, rescuing people whose eyes are beginning to glaze whether they're bored or drunk, and watching people's drinks.

One of the easiest ways is to mix a cocktail like a dry martini that can be carried round in a jug, or to give everyone wine, or to let people help themselves. Otherwise you'll get in a terrible muddle remembering what everyone wants and start giving them whisky and tonic and gin and soda.

GOING TO PARTIES

Don't stand together all evening, it will upset your hostess. Check every twenty minutes to ensure your partner isn't standing alone, doesn't need rescuing from the local bore, isn't pinned to the wall by the local sex maniac.

If you want to dance cheek to cheek with the most attractive woman in the room, wait until your wife is securely trapped on the sofa in another room.

If you catch your partner making a pass at someone, smile broadly as though it were an everyday occurrence, say, "Drink always takes him this way, he won't remember a thing about it next morning." Just the same, whisk him away smartly.

HOW TO LEAVE

There is bound to be a moment when you want to go home and your husband doesn't because he's

Overcome by lust

having too good a time, or *vice versa*. One of you will just have to grin and bear it. Don't get into the habit of leaving independently. It looks bad, and is very expensive on taxis.

If you're both bored, intimate to your hostess that you've been overcome by lust and must leave. She'll think her party has been a contributing factor and will be delighted.

THE OFFICE

OFFICE PARTIES

If husbands and wives aren't invited, be extremely careful. This is the moment when Mr. Chalcott in Accounts, who has been eying Mrs. Pointer in Personnel all the year, suddenly gets too much drink in him, makes a pass at her and the whole thing erupts into an affair. Try not to get home too late, be careful to wipe lipstick off your cheek if you're a man, and replace your make-up carefully if you're a woman. The fact that Mr. Prideau in Packaging saw fit to pounce on you may be just Christmas high spirits, but it will worry your husband, who'll think it is normal procedure for the rest of the year.

If you go to your wife's or husband's office party, be as nice as possible to everyone. These people may seem draggy to you, but your partner's got to put up with them all the year round, and will get tremendous kudos if you're a success.

Be prepared for anything—my mother went to my father's office party once when he was in a very senior position. She was hotly pursued by a man from the boiler division in a Mickey Mouse mask, who kept tracking her down in a corridor, tossing her up in the air, and crying, "I am your demon lover."

Hotly pursued

Be careful what you wear, look pretty but not outrageous. When I was newly married, I went to the Authors' Ball at the Hilton in a party of my husband's grandest business colleagues. Very brown from the south of France, I wore a white strapless dress which was so tight that I didn't need a bra. The five-course dinner was too much for it. As I stood up to dance with one of the directors, it split, leaving me naked to the waist.

OFFICE RELATIONSHIPS

A husband spends far more of his waking life with his secretary, and the people he works with, than with his wife. It is the same for his wife if she goes out to work. It is very easy to get crushes on people you work with. There's naturally proximity, there's the charm of the clandestine (we mustn't let anyone in the office know), of working together for a common purpose, and finally, because men basically like to boss, and women to be bossed, there is the fatal charm of the boss/female employee relationship. For if you are used to obeying a man when he says "Take a letter," or "Make me a cup of coffee," you may find it difficult to say no when he says "Come to bed with me."

Bear in mind before you either pounce, or accept the pounce across the desk, that people aren't nearly so easy to live with as to work with, and you'd probably be bored to death with your boss or secretary if you had to spend twenty-four hours a day with either one. It will also make things very awkward later if you go off them while they still fancy you, or vice versa. You may be forced to leave a job you like.

Be very careful, too, not to let your husband or wife think that you are keen on someone in the office, or your mate will go through agonies of jealousy during the day, and raise hell every time you are kept late—even if you are working.

HAVING YOUR HUSBAND'S BOSS TO DINNER

The wife should pull out all the culinary stops and look as beautiful as possible.

But don't flirt with your husband's boss too

much or you'll have him sending your husband abroad and coming round on his own!

Invite another amusing but socially reliable couple to meet him. Then when you and your husband have to leave the room to dish up or pour drinks, he won't be left alone to examine the damp patches or the peeling wallpaper.

Give him plenty to drink but not too much, or he may become indiscreet about company politics, regret it next day and take against your husband.

DINING OUT WITH YOUR HUSBAND'S BOSS

Can be terrifying, particularly when four of you sit down at a table big enough for twenty and your platitudes have to carry across eight feet of polished mahogany.

If you get paralyzed with nerves and can't think of a thing to say, your best bet is to laugh at everyone's jokes and look as though you're enjoying yourself.

Remarks like: "I don't know anything about reinforced concrete, do tell me," cover a multitude of inadequacies.

I remember when I was first married going out to dinner with a very distinguished authoress whom my husband, a publisher, was trying to impress.

As soon as I sat down in her livingroom, I leaped to my feet saying I hoped I hadn't taken her chair. "These are all my chairs," she said icily.

GENERAL MARITAL PROBLEMS

COMMUNICATION

One of the beauties of marriage is that you always have someone to look after, and to look after you, to share your problems, and to tell—without boasting—when something good happens to you.

It is vital that couples should get into the habit of talking to each other and be interested in each other's activities, be it a game of golf, an afternoon at the women's club, or a day at the office. If you are able to communicate on a daily level, you will find it much easier to discuss things when a major crisis blows up—like a husband losing his job, a sudden sexual impasse, or the television breaking down.

Nothing is more depressing than seeing married couples on vacation or dining together gazing drearily into space with nothing to say to one another—at best it's a shocking example to unmarried people.

I feel strongly that married women should try to set a good example to newlyweds or people about to get married. Nothing is more morale-lowering for the engaged girl than to be taken aside by a couple of bored and cynical married women and told how dreary marriage is, the only

Pregnancy

solution being infidelity or burying oneself in one's children. Rather in the same way that women who have children often terrorize women who are pregnant for the first time with hair-raising stories of childbirth.

SEPARATION

In long separations from your husband or wife, there are all the problems of loneliness and fidelity. Even short separations—a week or a week end— have their own difficulties.

When her husband goes away, a wife steels herself not to mind, and although she misses him, unconsciously she builds up other resources. She finds it is rather fun to read a novel until three o'clock in the morning, have time to get the house straight, watch what programs *she* wants on television, not have to cook and wash, and be able to see all the people she is not allowed to see when her husband is at home.

Gradually as the time for her husband's return approaches, she gets more and more excited. She plans a special homecoming dinner, she buys a new dress and goes on a twenty-four-hour diet so she will look beautiful. In her mind she has a marvelously idealized picture of his homecoming.

And then he arrives—hung over, grubby, exhausted, and if he's returning from where the time is different, he'll be absolutely knackered. He won't want to do anything else but fall into bed and then only to sleep.

The wife is inevitably disappointed—this is no god returning, merely a husband, grumbling about the ring around the bathtub, bringing not passion and tenderness but a suitcase of dirty shirts.

Similarly, a husband returning to his wife after some time away will find that an ecstatic welcome is often followed by a good deal of sniping and bad temper. The wife will have stored up so much unconscious resentment at being deprived of his presence, that she will take it out on him for a few days.

The only way to cope with *après*-separation situations is not to get panicky if your wife or husband acts strangely. It doesn't mean your spouse has met someone else; he is just taking a bit of time to adjust to your presence again. In a small way, it's like starting one's marriage over again.

ILLNESS

Men will react in the strangest way to illness. Some men take it in their stride when you're ill, and love the opportunity to fuss over you and bring you delicious food on trays. Some men are simply chaotic, as a friend said:

"All I got was gray poached eggs, swimming in water, and blackened bacon, and when I staggered down after forty-eight hours, I'd never seen such shambles in the kitchen—you'd think he'd been having forty people staying for a fortnight."

My husband, normally the most considerate and sensitive of men, reacts initially with rage and fury whenever I'm ill. He acts as though it's entirely my fault, and keeps muttering that I'm conspiring against him.

Recently, when I was rushed by him to a hospital for an emergency operation, he berated me during the entire drive until I was reduced to tears. Then he told me he wouldn't be able to visit me while I was laid up since he just couldn't abide hospitals. Of course, his reaction was due to panic

—he was worried sick and the only way he could relieve his anxiety was to hit out at someone, and the nearest person happened to be me. In fact, he never missed a visiting hour and simply couldn't have been more adorable and considerate. When I came home two weeks later, he nursed me angelically through six grim weeks of convalescence.

I only repeat this because, from talking to other women, I think a number of husbands react to stress in exactly the same way; where a woman would burst into tears, a man works himself into a rage. So if your husband loses his temper the next time you develop a migraine or an ingrown toenail, it's probably only because he's worried about you.

JEALOUSY

Once your life is centered around one person, it is very easy to become obsessively jealous. Try and keep your jealousy in check; it will only cause you suffering, and make things very difficult for your partner.

If you marry a very pretty girl, or a very attractive man, the fact has to be faced that people will still go on finding her or him attractive.

Give your wife a certain amount of rope, let her go out to lunch with other men, but start kicking up if it becomes a weekly occurrence with the same man. Never let her have drinks in the evening unless it's business or an old friend, and draw the line at breakfast.

Whenever I'm getting cozy with any man over thirty-five, my husband has an infuriating habit of coming over and treating the man with exaggerated courtesy, and asking him if he'd like to sit down and take the weight off his feet. If the admirer's under thirty-five, my husband will take the first opportunity of telling me he's queer as Dick's hatband.

A friend of mine has an infallible way of routing competition. When any woman her husband fancies is coming to dinner she always rings her up beforehand and tells her to wear something warm because the heating's broken down. By the time her rival gets there, however, the heating plant has made a miraculous recovery, and her uncomfortable guest spends the evening puce in the face and pouring with sweat.

If you are married to the sort of man who's always humiliating you by running after women at parties, you'll have to grin and bear it. He's probably just testing his sex appeal, like when gorillas beat their chests. Before I was married, a girlfriend and I used to divide men into open gazers, or secret doers. You've probably got an open gazer, so thank your lucky stars you're not married to a secret doer.

If you have an ex-wife or an ex-lover, destroy all

evidence before you get married again. Nothing is more distressing for a second wife than coming upon wedding photographs of you and your first wife looking idyllically happy.

However much you may want to reminisce about your exes, keep it to a minimum, and if you ever have to meet any of your wife's or husband's exes, be as nice to them as possible. No one looks attractive when sulking.

BOREDOM

It was not my intention in this book to deal with marriage in relation to children, but I would like to say a brief word about Cabbage-itis, which is my name for the slough of despond a wife goes through when she has two or more very young children to look after. Invariably she's stuck in the country or a part of town where she has few friends, her husband is going out to work every day and meeting interesting people and she isn't, and she feels dull, inadequate and so bored she could scream.

The family budget won't stretch to any new clothes for her, so she feels it is impossible for her to look attractive. On the occasions when friends bring children over for the day, it seems to be all chaos and clamor. She spends days planning a trip to town, which invariably ends in disappointment: her clothes are all wrong, she's worn out after two hours' shopping, the girlfriend she meets at lunch can't talk about anything except people she doesn't know, and if she attempts to take the children she's exhausted before she's begun.

She and her husband can't afford to entertain much, but when they are asked out she finds she is so used to saying "No" and "Don't" to children all day, she is unable to contribute to the conversation.

If you are going through this stage—and I think it is one of the real danger zones of marriage—remember that it isn't going on forever. The children will grow up, go to school, and you will have acres of free time to go back to work, to take up hobbies, to make new friends. Whatever you do, try not to let yourself go to seed. Looking pretty isn't new clothes, it's clean hair, a bit of make-up and a welcoming hug when your husband comes home in the evening.

Remember that your husband must always come first, even before the children. In your obsession with your domestic problems, it's possible to forget that he probably isn't having a very easy time either: desperately pushed for money, harassed at work, buffeted back and forth in a train every day, coming home to a drab, fractious wife every night.

It's better not to catalog your woes when he arrives in the evening. Concentrate on giving him a good time.

Try and go out at least once a week if it's only

to the movies. Try to read a newspaper, or at least listen to the news while you're doing the housework, so you won't feel too much out of touch.

If possible find something remunerative to do in the evening even if it's only making paper flowers, typing, or framing pictures. Nothing is more depressing than poverty and if you can make the smallest contribution to the family budget it will be a boost to your morale.

CLOTHES

CLOTHES AND APPEARANCE

"The reason why so few marriages are happy," said misogynist Swift, "is because young ladies spend their time in making nets, not in making cages."

I think it is very unwise for a wife to stop taking trouble over her appearance once she's married. She bothered enough to look pretty while she was trying to hook her husband, so it's a poor compliment to him if she slackens up immediately after he's hooked.

Remember that the world is full of pretty girls who are not averse to amorous dalliance, and if you want to keep your husband, you should make an effort to go on attracting him.

It's a case, of course, of shacking-up *à son goût*. Some men prefer their wives *au naturel*, others are like the husband who said to me: "The marvelous thing about old Sue is that she always looks as neat as a new pin. I've never seen her without make-up or slopping around in jeans."

Remember too that no man ever went off his wife because he saw a crowd of men around her. So always pull out the stops when you go to parties, or out in the evening, or pick your husband up at

Exotic clothes

the office. It is important to him that other people think you're attractive.

And even if your husband does prefer you without make-up, put some on when you go to a party. You'll have to compete with all those dollies with their wigs and falls and their three pairs of false eyelashes. Your husband won't be amused if he has to keep leaving the pretty girls he's chatting up to look after you because you've been abandoned.

If a wife wants to jazz up her husband's wardrobe, her best method is to start giving him exotic clothes for his birthday. He'll never go and buy them of his own accord.

It's nice if husbands and wives take an interest in each other's appearance. My husband's always thrilled to bits if I tell him he looks gorgeous, and even if a husband's the sort of man who can't tell a discarded false eyelash from a centipede, it's encouraging to his wife if he tells her she looks pretty when she's all dressed up to go out in the evening, or when she's wearing a new dress.

SEWING

Great row potential here.

Shirt buttons always fly off when the man is getting dressed in the morning, or last thing at night when you're both going to bed, so they never get sewn on. The wife will also plump for Banlon socks and say they are healthier and cheaper, and can be thrown away when they get holes, to be told by her husband that his mother always darned his woollen ones.

If the wife really can't sew, she should just content herself with sewing on buttons, and send all major repairs to the cleaners, where they can be done for a small charge.

VACATIONS

Much of the chapter on honeymoons applies here. People are so grimly determined to enjoy every moment of their vacations that they feel dismayed and cheated if anything goes wrong.

You're probably both exhausted, particularly if you've only been married a short time, and have had all the strain of getting adjusted. You've been planning and looking forward to your vacation for ages, then you arrive at your destination and find you're so unused to doing nothing that it takes you at least two weeks to unwind. Then it's time to go home again.

There is also the sex problem. Before you were married, vacations were always treated as safaris. The moment you boarded the train, the sap started rising, the eye started roving on the lookout for a vacation playmate. After you're married, the hunting instinct dies very hard. As a friend of mine said: "Taking a married man to the South of France is rather like taking a foxhound to a meet on a lead, and not letting him join in the chase."

I'm not a believer in retaliation but if your husband does get a crush on another girl on vacation —carrying her beachbag, always ready with a large towel when she comes up from the sea—your

Disastrous vacations

best answer rather than sulking is to take to the nearest gigolo. And if there isn't a gigolo to take, comfort yourself with the thought that holiday romances seldom last beyond the holiday.

Going on vacation with friends, of course, is one of the quickest ways of losing them. The most amiable people turn into absolute monsters when they've got too much spare time on their hands.

Everyone will either want to do different things (lying in the sun, sightseeing, skin diving, pony trekking, or merely getting drunk) or else no one will admit what they want to do, and go round looking martyred: "What would you like to do today, my darling?"

"Anything *you* like, darling."

"Oh don't be awkward."

Particularly avoid going with people who are

much richer than you (you'll worry the whole time about spending too much) or poorer than you (or you'll spend your time grumbling about their meanness).

We went to France once in a party of twelve, all great friends. It was a catastrophe. Meals were exactly like being back at school: "Hands up for *salade Niçoise*." All the people who could speak French pulled rank on the people who couldn't or didn't dare. All the wives sulked because all the husbands had gotten crushes on the one single girl, who was sulking because she couldn't hook the one single man. Bad will was absolutely rampant.

I am painting a gloomy picture of vacations because I think people often feel that if they've had a disastrous one their marriage must be on the rocks. "If we can't get on when we're on vacation," they say, "there must be something radically wrong." Forget it. Cheerful pessimism is the best approach to a vacation, and console yourself that the most disastrous vacations are always the funniest in retrospect.

HOW TO BEHAVE

On vacation there is invariably one who does the planning—booking rooms, tickets etc.—and one who resists being planned. If you're the resister, cut down on the beefing, whether it's about the lack of soap, coat-hangers, hot water, drawer space, or amount of garlic in the food. Remember, when in Rome . . . and shut up about it.

Don't overdo the sun—vacations are meant for lots of sex, and you won't feel like it if you wince every time you touch each other. And it's depressing to start peeling like a ticker-tape welcome as soon as you turn brown.

Travel is inclined to broaden the hips as well as the mind. Take a few shifts and larger-sized trousers.

Take lots of books and sleeping pills. One often can't sleep in hot countries, and nothing is more depressing than to feel that all the good of your vacation is being wasted because of insomnia. Take a reliable digestive remedy, too, so you won't spend all night thundering to the john.

Remember you won't be able to buy the Pill, or whatever you use, in a Catholic country. One couple were staying in a villa in Spain, and a particularly greedy guest came down one morning, found their contraceptive paste in the refrigerator, thought it was some exotic pâté and spread it on his toast for breakfast.

Go somewhere where there's something to do: a casino, night club, boats to sail, etc.

Money should be shared and watched over: nothing wrecks a vacation more quickly than the constant fear that you may run out of cash.

Husbands and wives should do their own packing to avoid endless recriminations about face cloths, slippers, razors, and cameras left behind.

It's horrible coming home to a dirty, untidy house. If you haven't got a cleaning woman, pay a chum a couple of dollars to come in the day before you get home to give the house a going-over.

Don't show slides. Don't bore everyone when you get back with stories of your vacation. My husband refuses to talk about it, and hangs a notice on his office door saying, "Yes."

SEX

BED

Bed/sex/intercourse/making love—call it what you like—is the cornerstone of marriage. If the sex side of a marriage is really good, you seldom hear of it breaking up. If you keep your partner happy in bed, he's unlikely to stray, and if he does he nearly always comes back.

Few people are born geniuses in bed—it is something you learn step by step, the way a child learns to talk. The first essential is to be honest with one another. Don't pretend to be going into ecstasies of excitement if you are not, or your partner will automatically assume he is doing the right things to please you, and keep on doing them.

A wife—if she can possibly help it—shouldn't pretend to be having an orgasm if she is not. Although her husband will flop down satisfied beside her afterwards, she will unconsciously build up a resentment both against him for not seeing through the cheat, and against herself for cheating.

Of course it's not vital to have an orgasm every time you go to bed with a man, but the fact remains that it's much nicer if you do. It draws you together, it gives you a marvelous feeling, and it's the best sleeping pill in the world.

Another myth that must be shattered is that men are lustful beasts whose appetites must be slaked, and women have to endure it.

"Your father was very good to me and never bothered me much," Victorian mothers used to tell daughters who were about to get married. "Just shut your eyes and think of England."

Recent research however has discovered that women can be just as highly sexed as men, need intercourse just as often, but in most instances are too inhibited to ask for it.

A wife should therefore not be ashamed to take a wholehearted enjoyment in sex, ask for it often, and if her husband isn't forthcoming, to seduce him, by making herself pretty, wearing sexy underwear, or simply by wandering round in the nude.

Don't be too fastidious. Nothing that two people who love each other do for their mutual enjoyment in the privacy of their own home can be wrong. If he's on a Lolita kick, pander to his whims and dress up in a gym tunic. If she's got a slave girl complex, tie her up and beat her before you make love to her.

Sex books are quite helpful but they always made us howl with laughter. They kept talking about the "upright male member," which made us think of an incorruptible M.P.

Read as much pornography as you can get your hands on, not only to excite you, but to give you ideas. Marriage needs every novelty to keep it

Nothing that two people do in their own home

going. A man I know said his wife was absolutely sensational in bed for at least a month after she'd read *Fanny Hill*.

For beginners (see the chapter on the honeymoon) the thing to remember is to take things slowly. It may be six months or a year before you manage to establish a sexual rapport. It's only in books that the man goes on drilling all night, and suddenly the rock splits and the oil comes gushing out. Enthusiasm is nine-tenths of the battle, plus perseverance. Kindness and gratitude are also essential. Tell your husband what doesn't work for you, but make pretty sure you tell him when it is good. If having the inside of your thighs stroked excites you, say so. Don't let him wait thirty years to find out.

Perservere with sex

HOW OFTEN

This is entirely up to you. Everyone lies about it if you ask them. I read in one book that the average man of thirty has sexual intercourse 2.8 times a week. When I told my husband, a rather smug gleam came into his eye, but he was curious to know what they did on the .8 occasion.

On the other hand, one Indian sex manual says that during the first year of marriage couples should have intercourse three times a night for the first three months, twice a night for the next three months, and every night for the rest of the year. After which I suppose you die of exhaustion.

There's no rule. Sometimes you may get a jag and have each other a dozen times in a week end, sometimes if you're both tired you may not feel like touching each other for a week or so.

HOW NOT TO LOOK IN BED
Curlers and great blobs of face cream are

Once a year

Making love to smelly people

grounds for divorce—no woman need wear them. If you want curly hair, get a set of heated rollers. If you want a soft skin, put on face cream in the bath.

People should wash and clean their teeth before they go to bed, and have at least one bath a day. This may sound elementary, but it's amazing how many people don't, and, sweat fetishists apart, most people would rather make love to someone who smells and tastes good.

Have separate beds if you must, but not separate rooms. Once you get accustomed to separate rooms, it's so easy to shut yourself in every night and grow further and further away from your partner. If one of you snores, or is a bad sleeper and wants to read, have a bed made up in the spare room, so you can slip into it if you get really desperate about three o'clock in the morning.

Don't, however, get out of the habit of making love. Quite often if you've been snapping at each other you will find that once you sleep together everything will be all right again.

I met a girl the other day who boasted she only gives herself to her husband once a year on his birthday. I think a woman should be grateful that her husband wants her, and that any woman who says, "I don't feel like it tonight," more than two days running, unless she's ill, very pregnant, or recovering from having a baby, is stirring up trouble for herself.

Equally, no man should continually refuse to sleep with his wife, if she obviously wants him. There's no excuse really for the sort of career man —American, as it happens—who will only sleep with his wife on Fridays and Saturdays, so he'll be fresh for work on weekdays.

Another of the great myths about sex is that for the first year you glut yourselves like someone working in a candy shop, and after that the glamour wears off and you settle down to pastimes like bringing up children and gardening. In any good marriage, sex should get better and better as the years go by, even if you indulge in it marginally less often.

AFFAIRS

Another great fallacy is that marriage stops you falling in love with people. It doesn't. One of the most happily married men I know says he was riddled with guilt because he developed a violent crush on a blonde staying in the same hotel while he was on honeymoon. If you were the sort of person who was always falling in love before marriage, you'll probably go on doing it afterwards. Don't panic—nip it in the bud early. Refuse to see the person concerned. It will tear your guts out for a few weeks, but you'll find you get over it, just as you got over the crushes you had before you were married.

If you suddenly find yourself fancying an attractive man, and you know he fancies you, don't try and rely on mutual self-control. One of the most short-sighted remarks ever made at the beginning of an affair is: "You're happily married and I'm happily married, and if we have an affair, we're both adult enough not to let it get out of hand, or let anyone get hurt." I'm afraid this is rubbish. Someone always gets hurt and it'll probably be you. Affairs, once allowed to begin, frequently get out of hand and can escalate into nasty things like divorce. Try to remember that once your husband finds out you're having an affair, it will cause him appalling unhappiness, and your marriage will never be the "glad confident morning" it was.

MUTUAL INFIDELITY

"Husbands are such a bore," said a friend of mine. "They always want to know whom you're dating." Some couples manage to go their own way, making a pledge of mutual infidelity, but I cannot help feeling that one of the partners must be enjoying it more than the other.

If you must have affairs, be discreet. The cardinal sin is to be found out. And when it's all over and you're feeling a louse and you want to clear your conscience, don't indulge in tearful confessions to your husband and feel you've cleaned the slate. It will upset him quite unnecessarily.

DISCOVERY

If you do discover your husband is having an affair with someone, and he doesn't know you know, play it cool. It may blow over. Remember, "the robb'd that smiles steals something from the thief."

If you find out, and your partner knows you know, the only solution is to raise hell, and insist that it stop immediately. Once you start condoning something like this, you're lost. Usually the jolt of your finding out and minding so much is enough to make him give up the other person, in which case welcome him home like the prodigal son, and *never never* reproach him again.

People often have affairs as a bid for more attention from their partners and purposely leave clues so that their partners will find out and be jolted into loving them more. So if you discover your husband is having an affair with someone, have a look at your own behavior before you blame him, to see if it's you who's at fault.

A FEW PRACTICAL SUGGESTIONS

If your wife seems like a bolter, put her on your own passport; then you won't waste a fortune in air tickets getting her back.

If you suspect your partner is having an affair with a particular person, go into howls of immoderate laughter every time that person's name is mentioned. When they ask why you're laughing, laugh some more and say no one takes that idiot seriously. Nothing douses passion quicker than ridicule. I really fancied a man once, until someone pointed out he looked like Dracula.

DETECTION

There are a number of indications that your

partner is having an affair with someone:

If your husband insists he's been lunching at the local with the boys, and comes home reeking of garlic, gets out a packet of matches with The Cozy Nook Motel printed on it, and lights a king-size cigarette when he normally smokes Camels . . .

If he starts a pointless row at breakfast, so he can storm out of the house, and needn't come back until late . . .

If he suddenly starts working late consistently and comes home smelling of perfume . . .

If he looks happy on Monday morning, and miserable on Friday night . . .

If he suddenly starts having a bath in the morning . . .

If the distance between the ends of his tie is different in the evening from the morning . . .

If he keeps making ridiculous excuses to buy more cigarettes during the week end when there are plenty in the house . . .

If there's a rash of wrong numbers, it may not be burglars . . .

If he starts bringing home flowers and expensive presents and it isn't your birthday, it's possible he's suffering from a guilty conscience . . .

If your wife after always dressing scruffily for the office suddenly starts smartening herself up, shaving her legs, buying new lingerie, and getting home late . . .

If she doesn't look dismayed when you say

If the cat isn't hungry

you're going abroad for three weeks . . .

If she is home all day and the toilet seat is up when you get home . . .

If she suddenly gets sexually revved up. Women are like machines, the more they're used the better they work . . .

If she starts suggesting you make love to her standing on your head, she may *not* have been reading the *Kama Sutra* . . .

If she starts leaving intellectual books by the bed, or tidying the house frantically in the morning . . .

If you have a man friend to stay, and he knows where to put things away when he's helping with the dishes . . .

If you're both out at work and you come home and find the towels all tidy in the bathroom instead of scrumpled-up, as usual. Or if the cat isn't hungry . . .

COMING UNSTUCK

Everyone can make a mistake, and there's no point in a couple sticking together if they're miserable, even for the sake of the children, who would be much happier with one contented parent than two continually at war. Do try and distinguish, however, between a temporary bad patch, which all marriages go through, and a permanent rift. Divorce is very unpleasant and very expensive. A great deal of mud-slinging and bitterness will inevitably occur, and there's the nasty business of dividing friends and property.

So before you run off, whether it's with someone or not, make absolutely sure you want to go. Your partner may or may not take you back afterwards, and the longer you stay away the more difficult it will be to start again.

Another thing to remember is that it's very cold outside the matrimonial cage. One beautiful woman I know recently left her husband because she was bored and unhappy. She was back within six months.

When she was safely married, she had a wonderful time, having numerous affairs, being hotly pursued by hordes of men (for nothing is more attractive to a man than a bored, beautiful but safely married woman—all fun and no fear). Once she had left her husband the men who had been swarming around her weren't nearly so anxious to declare themselves, and she soon found it was back to single-girl status with all the nagging worries of who was going to take her out the next night.

Sometimes an affair can ventilate a marriage and make a couple appreciate each other more:

Another friend of mine became so infatuated with her lover that she left her husband. Next morning she and her lover went along to the lover's lawyer, who asked her if there was anything detrimental they could use against her husband in the divorce. Was he cruel? Did he neglect her? Did he have affairs with other women or beat her up?

She thought for a minute and then burst into tears, saying she couldn't think of anything wrong with him. She rushed out of the office and went back to her husband, whom to her amazement she found absolutely devastated by her departure. They have been happily married ever since.

BREEDING

"Has Tom fertilized Wendy yet?" asked one of the small bridesmaids gazing at the bridal couple at a recent wedding.

Premature certainly, but it's amazing how many brides have to carry extra large bouquets these days.

A girl I know who was married when she was eight months pregnant was given a year's subscription to a diaper service by her office as a wedding present. Although there will be a few raised eyebrows if a baby turns up before nine months have elapsed, particularly if it is a spanking ten pounder and cannot be fobbed off as premature, the fact remains that the moment you get back from your honeymoon, people will start expecting you to get pregnant.

Every time the wife looks tired, has an upset stomach or leaves a party early, people will start exchanging knowing looks.

If after two years nothing happens, the pressure will really be on. Hints are dropped about "getting set in your ways," or "too used to living on two incomes." People will keep suggesting you move to the country and send you real estate agents' lists of suburban homes with large gardens. Dire warn-

An extra large bouquet

ings will be given about the difficulty of having babies after the age of twenty-five.

After three years, you will be offered names of "perfectly marvelous gynecologists," and friends will say the wife is overtiring herself and ought to give up work. People will take her aside and say: "Don't you think Henry ought to see a doctor as well, darling?"

Parents-in-law will display angst about not having any grandchildren to talk about at bridge parties.

They should all realize that it's none of their business. Anyone who starts interfering on this subject deserves a flea in the ear.

If couples don't have children, it's either because they don't want to yet, or because they're trying and they can't. Not being able to have children, whether it's temporary or permanent, is extremely distressing. (There is something tragic and yet ridiculous about those abortive threshings night after night.) Outsiders should not contribute to this distress by asking stupid questions.

I couldn't have children and, after seven traumatic years of trailing from doctor to doctor, we finally in extreme trepidation adopted one. It has been an unqualified success. Within twenty-four hours of the child's arrival we were infatuated with him, and couldn't imagine life without him.

The month before the baby arrived was the most difficult I've had ever had to live through. Everyone told us we were too set in our ways.

"You are going to have your hands full, you don't know what hard work is until you've got a baby," they would say to me. "No more lying in bed until lunchtime, no more parties every night. You'll miss the intellectual stimulus of your job, won't you, and aren't you going to be very short of money?"

I timidly said I intended to freelance as a journalist.

"Freelance!! My dear, you won't have a moment, and even if you do, you'll be far too physically exhausted to tackle anything mental."

Neither were they backward in coming forward with an avalanche of advice. All conflicting. The battles that raged between the bottle boilers and the non-boilers, those who used disposable diapers and those who preferred the diaper service. Everyone gave me wildly differing lists of what I should need for the baby.

I bought several baby books and found them unreadable. Every time I sat down with one, it would fall open at vomiting or green movements. I never got beyond the first chapter.

My husband, however, was fascinated by the section on husbands' reactions.

"It says I'm going to feel left out," he read happily, "and I'll express it by feeling grumpy toward you, wanting to spend more evenings with my men friends and by flirting with other women."

In fact he was marvelous the whole time. Having one child already from a previous marriage, he knows all about babies, and was able to tell me exactly what to do when the baby arrived.

The first week on my own was a bit nerve-racking, I was so brainwashed by what everyone had told me, I even found myself sterilizing the cat's plates. But I soon found that, contrary to all the rubbish that's talked, young babies take up very little of one's time.

For the first twelve months we had the baby, I managed to run a sizable house, look after the baby all myself, and pack in at least six hours' writing a day. Now that he's older, I have a baby sitter who takes him off my hands in the afternoon, so I can work. Yet I know mothers who have a nurse and a maid in the house and are worn to a frazzle with worry, waking their babies up every five minutes to see if they're all right.

Or like my mother, who came roaring into my father's study when I was a baby saying:

"I shall have to sack Nanny, she was two minutes late with Jilly's orange juice."

Babies pick up tension like radar, and the more you worry and fret over them, the more tense and difficult they become, until they don't sleep at night, and then you don't sleep because you're worrying about them, and get even more exhausted and bad tempered during the day, which makes the child even worse and the whole thing becomes a vicious circle. This is why second babies are generally so much more placid; the mother hasn't got so much time on her hands for worrying.

My husband's theory is that if a baby is going to be a joy rather than a burden to a marriage, you must impose your routine on him, rather than him imposing his routine on you.

The first few days after our baby arrived, whenever he cried at night, I was out of bed like a greyhound released from the slips, but each time my husband grabbed me and forcibly held me down. Invariably after I'd suffered two or three lacerating moments listening to the baby's wails, the baby would fall asleep again. Soon he virtually stopped waking, and since then we've never had a sleepless night with him.

Equally during the day when I was working, if he cried I seldom heard him above the thunder of the typewriter, so he learned to play quite happily in his crib while waiting for his next feeding.

This may sound both smug and heartless, but you couldn't find a more placid, jolly baby. He's immensely sociable, loves meeting new people, and hates being dragged away from a party.

One of the great revelations of my life was how immeasurably much better life was when one was married than unmarried. Another was how much better marriage is when one has children.

CONCLUSION

I am fully aware of the inadequacies of this book. Some aspects of marriage are covered very scantily and some not at all, and because I was writing about staying married, I have dwelt more on the pitfalls than on the very considerable joys of marriage.

"For everyone, and particularly for women and children," Cecil King wrote recently, "the essential basis for security and happiness is a loving home."

Marriage is not a battlefield, it is a partnership, and married people should be partners, not rivals. And although it is important to be a reliable bread-winner, a splendid cook, a good manager, and magnificent in bed, the most priceless gift one married person can give to another is a merry and a loving heart.